scjc

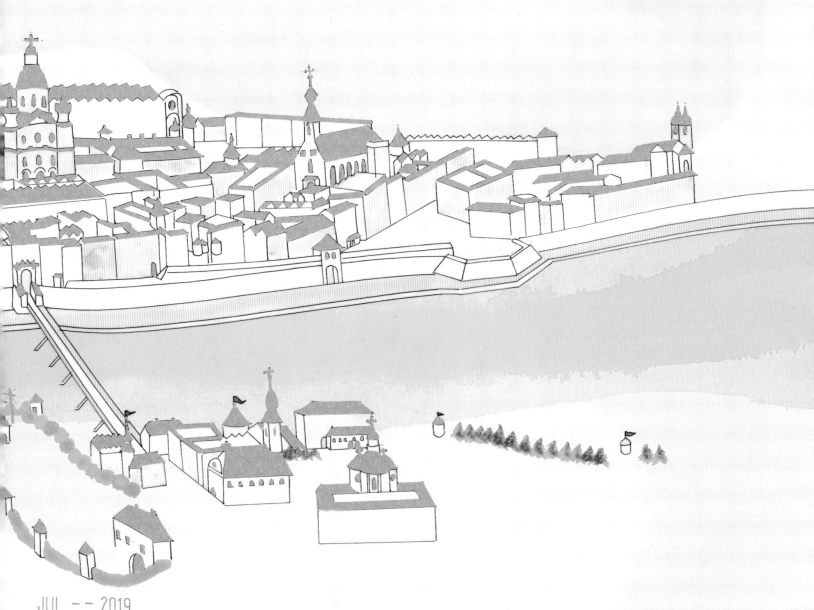

Mozart
Gift of God

For children of all ages and for Wolfgang Amadeus Mozart, who is music.
Demi

I always have God before my eyes.
I acknowledge His omnipotence, I dread His wrath;
but I also know His love, His compassion
and mercy towards His creatures,
and that He will never forsake His servants.
When His will is done I am resigned;
so I never can fail to be happy.

Wolfgang Amadeus Mozart

Mozart
Gift of God

Written
and illustrated by

DEMI

MAGNIFICAT • Ignatius

Wolfgang Amadeus Mozart was one of the world's most gifted musicians. From early childhood, his talents amazed everyone—even the royalty of Europe. His glorious works filled his listeners with wonder, as they still do today.

Wolfgang was born in Salzburg, Austria, on January 27, 1756. His father, Leopold, was a concertmaster for the city's prince-archbishop.

His mother, Anna Maria, lovingly cared for her home and family.

Mozart's sister, Maria Anna (whose nickname was "Nannerl"), was five years older than Wolfgang. She was musically gifted too.

When Leopold was teaching Nannerl the harpsichord, little Wolfgang, only three years old, imitated the lessons. Soon Leopold was tutoring Wolfgang too. The boy quickly mastered the harpsichord, the violin, and the organ. By the time he was five, he was composing his own music, which his father wrote down in a notebook.

The Mozarts were Roman Catholics, and their faith played a central role in their lives.

The family said daily prayers and attended Sunday Mass.

They fasted during Lent, and they happily celebrated the Church's many feast days.

In 1762, Father and Mother Mozart decided to share their child prodigies with the world. The family traveled to Munich, Vienna, and Prague, where six-year-old Wolfgang and eleven-year-old Nannerl skillfully played multiple instruments. The dazzled audiences called them *Wunderkinder* (wonder children).

In Vienna, the Mozarts performed at the Schönbrunn Palace of the Habsburgs, who ruled over an important part of Europe. Empress Maria Theresa, who had ten children of her own, was very impressed by Nannerl and Wolfgang. At the end of the concert, Wolfgang jumped onto the royal lap and gave the empress a big kiss. She did not scold the boy for bad manners but laughed with delight.

The Mozart family took several more trips, and Wolfgang inspired awe wherever they went.

The boy could expertly play a keyboard with his hands hidden beneath a cloth. He could name a note played on any instrument, including bells, glasses, and clocks. He could improvise sublime pieces on the organ and play them for as long as his listeners desired.

In France, the Mozarts performed at the palace of Versailles. Wolfgang enchanted the entire court and charmed the royal children. He composed a sonata for Victoire de France, the daughter of King Louis XV.

In 1764, the Mozarts traveled to London, where the children played for King George III and Queen Charlotte. Wolfgang later wrote a set of violin sonatas dedicated to the queen.

While in London, Wolfgang studied under Johann Christian Bach. After hearing some of Bach's symphonies, Wolfgang wrote one too. He also composed his first opera. A famous tenor said that he would never forget the boy's face "lighted up with the glowing rays of genius. It is as impossible to describe as it would be to paint sunbeams."

Traveling was very hard in those days. In the Netherlands, Wolfgang and Nannerl caught typhoid fever, and it took many months for them to recover.

While the Mozarts were visiting Vienna in 1767, a smallpox epidemic broke out. The family fled the city, but Nannerl and Wolfgang came down with the dreaded disease. Thankfully, they both survived.

After the danger was over, the Mozarts returned to Vienna. By this time, Wolfgang was twelve years old and writing all kinds of music.

When asked about his composing, Mozart pointed to his ear, his head, and his heart and said that music came to him as a gift.

Under the guidance of his father, Wolfgang's God-given talents were perfected by study and hard work. Over the course of his life, he produced hundreds of extraordinary pieces that have influenced all styles of music.

At age thirteen, Wolfgang wrote his first major piece of sacred music, the *Te Deum*, a hymn of praise to God.

"I always have God before my eyes," he later wrote to his father.

"I acknowledge His omnipotence, I dread His wrath; but I also know His love, His compassion and mercy towards His creatures."

*I*n 1770, Wolfgang's father took him on a grand tour of Italy. The fourteen-year-old met the pope in Rome and many famous musicians throughout the country.

The court of Milan paid Wolfgang to write his first serious opera, *Mithridates, King of Pontus*, which was performed to great acclaim.

While in Italy, Mozart went by the name Wolfgango Amadeo. Amadeo means "lover of God." It is the Italian form of his middle name Theophilus. When he returned to Austria, he was forever known as Wolfgang Amadeus Mozart.

Sixteen-year-old Mozart was hired by the prince-archbishop of Salzburg to work as a concertmaster beside his father. Over the next several years, he wrote numerous symphonies, concertos, Masses, and other works.

Not appreciating his towering genius, the prince-archbishop treated Wolfgang like a servant. His father took him to other cities in search of commissions, but the prince-archbishop frowned upon this.

After Wolfgang turned twenty-one, he left Salzburg with his mother to try his luck elsewhere.

"Lamb of God, You take away the sins of the world."

Mozart told a friend that, as he set these words to music, he could feel what they mean. "I have been initiated from earliest childhood in the mystical sanctuary of our religion," he said. There, one "waits with a heart full of devotion for the divine," receives the Eucharist, and "rises lightened and uplifted."

Wolfgang and his mother ended up in Paris, where work was hard to come by. After his mother died, Wolfgang sadly returned to Salzburg. The prince-archbishop hired him again, but Mozart was more miserable than before. He quarreled often with his employer, who eventually fired him with a kick in the pants.

During his travels, Wolfgang met Aloysia Weber, a beautiful and talented soprano.
Mozart adored her and wrote music for her, but she did not return his affections.
When he learned that she had married someone else, he was heartbroken.

He did not stay heartbroken for long, however. He fell in love again—this time with Aloysia's younger sister, Constanze. The two of them were married on August 4, 1782, at Saint Stephen's Cathedral in Vienna.

The newlyweds were very happy. A singer like her sister, Constanze shared her husband's passion for music. Mozart had plenty of work, and his music soared to new heights.

The household was a merry one. They had pets, hosted parties, and played games. Yet Mozart composed constantly.

When Wolfgang's father visited the young couple, the famous composer Joseph Haydn told him, "Before God and as an honest man, I tell you that your son is the greatest composer known to me." Like Haydn, Mozart often prayed the Rosary.

$\mathcal{M}$ozart described how his music came to him. He said that when he was completely relaxed, when traveling in a carriage for example, melodies arose in his mind—as if he could hear instruments playing. Later, he would write the pieces down and revise them until they were perfect.

In 1786, Mozart's opera *The Marriage of Figaro* premiered in Vienna. The lively romantic comedy was well received, and it is a favorite of opera fans to this day.

The production was an even bigger hit in Prague, where it was called "a masterpiece" and proof of Mozart's "divine inspiration."

Wolfgang was greatly admired in Prague. He traveled there quite a bit for many successful productions of his music.

*M*ozart next wrote *Don Giovanni*, one of the greatest operas of all time.

As Mozart worked on it, he learned that his father was deathly ill. To encourage him, he wrote a letter saying that death is the "true goal of our life" and a "faithful friend of man."

Wolfgang could say such things because he believed that Christ died to give mankind eternal life. This faith gave him much joy. "I daily thank my Creator for such a happy frame of mind," he also wrote his father, "and wish from my heart that every one of my fellow-creatures may enjoy the same."

*A*ll told, Mozart wrote twenty-two operas full of colorful characters.

The Magic Flute is Mozart's most playful yet profound opera. He wrote it in 1791, the last year of his life.

The crowds loved the fantastic fairy tale—with its magic, love, humor, and high ideals.

While Mozart was composing *The Magic Flute*, money was very tight. Mozart accepted every job that came his way and worked feverishly day and night. He became very sick, and still he kept on working.

He wrote two other operas, a piano concerto, a string quintet, and a clarinet concerto. For the feast of Corpus Christi, he wrote the magnificent *Ave Verum Corpus*, in praise of the Eucharist.

His last and unfinished piece was a requiem, a funeral Mass. The person who requested it did not identify himself, but he offered to pay handsomely. Weakened and bedridden, Wolfgang came to believe he was writing the requiem for himself.

On December 5, 1791, Wolfgang died. He was only thirty-five years old, the father of two young children.

He received the plainest of burials, as was the custom in Vienna for ordinary citizens. His shocked and grieving wife was too weak to attend.

Five days later, a beautiful funeral Mass was celebrated for Mozart at Saint Michael's Church. It was paid for by a friend. Some of Vienna's most accomplished musicians volunteered to perform the completed parts of Mozart's *Requiem*, in honor of one of the greatest composers the world has ever known.

Truly, his music was a gift from God.

Under the direction of Romain Lizé, Executive Vice President, MAGNIFICAT

Editor, MAGNIFICAT: Isabelle Galmiche
Editor, Ignatius: Vivian Dudro
Proofreader: Kathleen Hollenbeck
Assistant to the Editor: Pascale van de Walle
Layout Designer: Gauthier Delauné
Production: Thierry Dubus, Sabine Marioni

Printed in compliance with the Consumer Protection Safety Act, 2008.

Printed in Malaysia by Tien Wah Press in January 2019
Job number MGN19002